Frankly, I NEVER WANTED TO KISS ANYBODY!

The Story of **THE FROG PRINCE**

as Told by **THE FROG**

by Nancy Loewen

illustrated by Denis Alonso

PICTURE WINDOW BOOKS
a capstone imprint

Special thanks to our adviser, Terry Flaherty, PhD, Professor of English, Minnesota State University, Mankato, for his expertise.

⋅∘⋅⚬🙐✕🙒⚬⋅∘⋅

Editor: Jill Kalz
Designer: Lori Bye
Art Director: Nathan Gassman
Production Specialist: Jennifer Walker
The illustrations in this book were created digitally.

⋅∘⋅⚬🙐✕🙒⚬⋅∘⋅

Picture Window Books
1710 Roe Crest Drive
North Mankato, MN 56003
www.capstonepub.com

Library of Congress Cataloging-in-Publication Data
Cataloging-in-publication information is on file with the Library of Congress.
ISBN 978-1-4048-8304-8 (library binding)
ISBN 978-1-4795-1948-4 (paper over board)
ISBN 978-1-4795-1952-1 (paperback)
ISBN 978-1-4795-1895-1 (eBook PDF)

Printed in the United States of America
in Stevens Point, Wisconsin.
082013   007684R

"You have to kiss a lot of frogs to find your prince."

I bet you've heard that one before. And I bet you're thinking—

EEEWWWWW!

Kissing a frog would be gross!

Well, I just happen to be the former frog who inspired that saying. My name is Prince Puckett. And let me tell you, that kiss was no picnic for me either! Here's the REAL story.

THE FROG PRINCE

I was playing baseball the day Hank's mom turned me into a frog. One moment I was about to catch Hank's pop fly—which would give my team the championship—

4

and the next moment I was flopping around on the ground with more legs than I knew what to do with.

"Sorry, kid," Hank's mom called as she was led out of the ballpark. "To break the spell, just get a princess to kiss you. But she can't know you're a prince!"

Well, whether I was a prince or a frog, I wasn't about to kiss any girl. And I soon found that being a frog had its perks.

I could see almost all the way around my head.

I could swim and dive like nobody's business.

And boy, could I jump!

I jumped and jumped all the way to a new home, near a well under an old linden tree.

One day I was playing kick-the-mushroom with my frog buddies when I heard the unmistakable sound of a ball smacking into a glove.

"That's the princess," Mickey told me. "She's always coming out here to practice."

I listened to the **smack ... smack ... smack.**
And I wished that I could be just a regular
baseball-playing prince again.

Then it happened.

Smack ... smack ... PLUNK!

The ball landed in the well.

"That was my lucky ball!" the princess cried.

The gang gathered around me. "If you offer to get the ball, she'll offer to pay you back somehow," Willie said. "Then you can ask for that kiss."

"Go on," Harmon prodded. "Think of your teammates back home."

11

I worked up my courage and jumped beside her.

"Would you like me to get your ball?" I asked.

"You?" she asked. "Well, I guess it wouldn't hurt to try."

I hopped into the well and kicked the ball out.

"How can I ever repay you?" the princess asked.
"Just ask and it's yours!"

"You can ... I mean ... I'd like a ...," I stammered.
Finally I blurted out,

"A kiss! I want you to kiss me!"

"Bleh!" the princess said.

We stared at each other.

She leaned toward me.

I leaned toward her.

"Nope, can't do it!" she said.
She took her ball and ran away.

Well, that made me a little mad. A deal's a deal, right?

It took me awhile, but jump by jump I followed her back to her castle.

The princess wouldn't open the door, but I stood there croaking loudly until her father, the king himself, let me in. I told him about our agreement.

"My daughter must keep her word,"
the king assured me in a booming voice.

Then he plopped me down on the dinner table, right next to her.

The princess looked the other way. "I'll kiss you after we eat,"
she said. "Promise."

But as soon as she'd swallowed her last bite of lemon tart, she dashed up the stairs.

I hopped right after her.

"I'll kiss you right before I go to sleep," she said. But she pulled the covers over her head and quickly began to fake snore.

I spotted her lucky ball in the corner. "Well, I guess I'll be going now," I said. "Since you won't kiss me, I'll just be taking this."

The princess flung off the covers. "No! Wait! I'll do it!"

She picked me up and held me to her face.

She closed her eyes.

I closed my eyes.

Then—her lips touched mine. **"UGH!"** we both shrieked.

I felt myself being hurled into the air. And suddenly
I was stumbling around with two legs and two arms
that I didn't know what to do with.

"You're a prince!" she said.

"What an arm!" I said.

Did we fall in love, get married, and live happily ever after?

NO WAY. But my team got a great new starting pitcher!

Critical Thinking Using the Common Core

If the princess told the story instead of the frog prince, how would her point of view differ? What details might she tell differently? (Craft and Structure)

Describe what happens in the story, considering these questions: How does the prince get turned into a frog, and what does he like about being a frog? Why does he decide he would rather go back to being a prince? What steps does he take to do so? What is the role of the princess' father as a character in the story? (Key Ideas and Details)

Look online to find the original story, and describe how the ending of this version of the story differs. Why might the author have chosen to change it? (Integration of Knowledge and Ideas)

Glossary

character—a person, animal, or creature in a story
point of view—a way of looking at something
version—an account of something from a certain
    point of view

Read More

Blair, Eric. *The Frog Prince: A Retelling of the Grimms' Fairy Tale*. My First Classic Story. Mankato, Minn.: Picture Window Books, 2011.

Bradman, Tony. *The Frog Prince Hops to It*. After Happily Ever After. Mankato, Minn.: Stone Arch Books, 2009.

Hopkins, Jackie. *The Horned Toad Prince*. Atlanta: Peachtree, 2000.

Internet Sites

FactHound offers a safe, fun way to find Internet sites related to this book. All of the sites on FactHound have been researched by our staff.

Here's all you do:
Visit *www.facthound.com*
Type in this code: 9781404883048

Look for all the books in the series:

Believe Me, Goldilocks Rocks!

Frankly, I Never Wanted to Kiss Anybody!

Honestly, Red Riding Hood Was Rotten!

No Kidding, Mermaids Are a Joke!

No Lie, I Acted Like a Beast!

Really, Rapunzel Needed a Haircut!

Seriously, Cinderella Is SO Annoying!

Seriously, Snow White Was SO Forgetful!

Truly, We Both Loved Beauty Dearly!

Trust Me, Jack's Beanstalk Stinks!

Super-cool stuff!

Check out projects, games and lots more at
www.capstonekids.com